CHICAGO
BLACKHAWKS

BY TODD KORTEMEIER

Book design by Maggie Villaume
Cover design by Maggie Villaume

Photographs ©: Mike Wulf/Cal Sport Media/ZUMA Wire/AP Images, cover; Elise Amendola/AP Images, 4–5, 7; Michael Tureski/Icon Sportswire, 8–9; Bettmann/Getty Images, 10–11; Bruce Bennett/Getty Images Studios/Getty Images, 13; AP Images, 15, 16–17; Les/AP Images, 18–19; Jonathan Kirn/AP Images, 21; Edward Kitch/AP Images, 23; Robin Alam/Icon Sportswire, 24–25; Matt Slocum/AP Images, 27; Matthew Pearce/Icon Sportswire, 29

Press Box Books, an imprint of Press Room Editions.

ISBN
978-1-63494-489-2 (library bound)
978-1-63494-515-8 (paperback)
978-1-63494-566-0 (epub)
978-1-63494-541-7 (hosted ebook)

Library of Congress Control Number: 2022902274

Distributed by North Star Editions, Inc.
2297 Waters Drive
Mendota Heights, MN 55120
www.northstareditions.com

Printed in the United States of America
082022

ABOUT THE AUTHOR

Todd Kortemeier is a sportswriter, children's book author, and die-hard Blackhawks fan. He and his wife live near the Twin Cities in Minnesota with their daughter and dog.

TABLE OF
CONTENTS

1

Patrick Kane
handles the puck
during Game 6 of
the 2013 Stanley
Cup Final.

SEVENTEEN SECONDS

Chicago Blackhawks goalie Corey Crawford raced toward the bench. On came an extra skater for Chicago. He joined the attack being led by forward Patrick Kane. The Hawks trailed the Boston Bruins by a score of 2–1. Less than 90 seconds remained in Game 6 of the 2013 Stanley Cup Final. The Hawks led the series three games to two. And they didn't want the series to go to Game 7.

Kane stickhandled past two Bruins. He fired a shot, but Boston's goalie deflected it. The puck rattled around in the corner. Hawks defenseman Duncan Keith gained control. He sent a pass to Jonathan Toews down low. Then Toews passed it to left wing Bryan Bickell, who was lurking in front of the goal. Bickell buried the puck in the back of the net. The game was tied!

The Boston crowd fell silent. Three games in the series had already gone to

RED-HOT HAWKS

The 2012–13 Blackhawks had one of the best starts to a season in history. Chicago earned at least one point in each of its first 24 games. Twenty-one of those games were wins. The Hawks had also earned at least a point in each of the final six games of the previous season. That streak of 30 games was the second longest ever.

Bryan Bickell (29) ties the game with only 1:16 remaining in the third period.

overtime. It looked like there would be a fourth.

Shortly after the face-off, the Hawks gathered a loose puck. Forward Dave Bolland brought it into the offensive zone.

Seconds later, Hawks defenseman Johnny Oduya unloaded a shot from near the blue line. The puck deflected off a teammate and hit the post. Bolland was right there. He blasted the puck into a wide-open goal. The Hawks now led 3–2! Only 17 seconds had passed since their last goal.

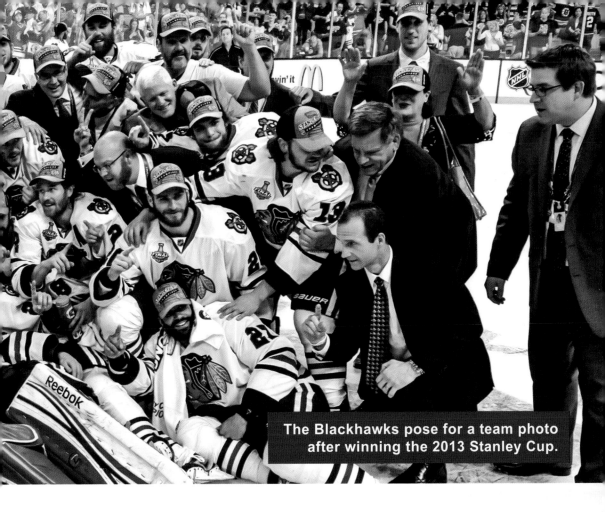

The Blackhawks pose for a team photo after winning the 2013 Stanley Cup.

Chicago held off Boston for the game's final minute. As the horn sounded, Blackhawks players streamed onto the ice and celebrated. Chicago had just won its second Stanley Cup in four years. It was another thrilling moment in a remarkable run of success.

2

The Chicago
Black Hawks take
on the Montreal
Maroons in the
early years of the
National Hockey
League.

THE FIRST CUPS

The National Hockey League (NHL) formed in 1917. In its first few years, the league included only Canadian teams. But in the 1920s, several US cities got teams. Chicago was one of them. The Black Hawks formed in 1926.

Team owner Frederic McLaughlin had served in the US Army during World War I (1914–1918). His unit was named after Black Hawk, a leader of the

Sauk people. McLaughlin decided to use the name for his hockey team.

Charlie Gardiner was one of the team's biggest stars in the early years. Gardiner was an excellent netminder. In 1932, he won the Vezina Trophy as the league's best goalie. He won it again in 1934. Gardiner also led the Hawks to the Stanley Cup Final that year.

Forwards Doc Romnes, Johnny Gottselig, and Paul Thompson were

THE CURSE OF MULDOON

Frederic McLaughlin fired Chicago head coach Pete Muldoon after the team's first season. Muldoon had led the team to the playoffs. But McLaughlin thought the team should have been better. Muldoon reportedly said the Hawks would never finish in first place. For the next 40 years, the "Curse of Muldoon" came true.

Charlie Gardiner served as Chicago's goalie from 1927 to 1934.

other key members of that Stanley Cup team. Romnes was the top scorer in the Final against the Detroit Red Wings. He assisted on the winning goal in double overtime to win the championship.

Meanwhile, Gardiner recorded a shutout in the game. Sadly, Gardiner died just two months later. He was only 29 years old.

Chicago made it back to the Stanley Cup Final in 1938. Led by captain Gottselig, the Hawks captured their second title.

The Black Hawks reached another Final in 1944, but this time they lost. That season marked the end of an era. McLaughlin died later in the year, and

Black Hawks players celebrate with coach Bill Stewart after winning the Stanley Cup in 1938.

the team didn't fare as well under new ownership. From 1945 through 1958, Chicago made the playoffs only twice.

3

Bobby Hull celebrates after winning the Stanley Cup in 1961.

RETURN TO GLORY

The Black Hawks changed owners again in 1954. This time, the team was led by James Norris and Arthur Wirtz. They had previously been part owners of the Detroit Red Wings. At the time, the Red Wings were one of the best teams in hockey. Norris and Wirtz were determined to make the Black Hawks just as good. So, they hired Detroit's head coach, Tommy Ivan.

Ivan had a great eye for talent. Under his watch, the Hawks acquired forwards Bobby Hull and Stan Mikita. They also got defenseman Pierre Pilote and goalie Glenn Hall. With this core of players, the Hawks improved quickly. By 1961, they were in the Stanley Cup Final.

Hull led the way as one of the most exciting forwards in the league. He was a speedy player.

Bobby Hull scores a goal against the Detroit Red Wings in 1963.

His flowing blond hair gave him the nickname "The Golden Jet." Hull paired that speed with a brutal slap shot.

In the 1961 playoffs, the Hawks upset the mighty Montreal Canadiens in the first round. Montreal had won the previous five Stanley Cups. Next, the Hawks blew away the Red Wings in the Final. It was Chicago's first title since 1938.

That group of Black Hawks reached four more Finals but lost them all. As the legends retired, new ones took their

THE NOISY ANTHEM

Chicago needed a boost in the 1985 playoffs. The team returned home down two games to none against the Edmonton Oilers. Fans started cheering during "The Star-Spangled Banner." After that, cheering during the anthem became a tradition. Now it happens at every home game.

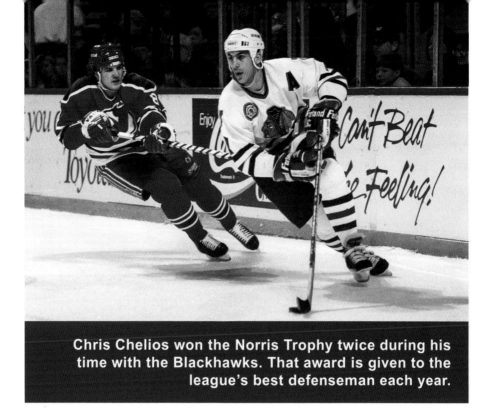

Chris Chelios won the Norris Trophy twice during his time with the Blackhawks. That award is given to the league's best defenseman each year.

place. And in 1986, the team changed the spelling of its name to "Blackhawks."

Defenseman Chris Chelios helped Chicago establish a physical style of play in the 1990s. Meanwhile, forward Jeremy Roenick drove a scoring attack. The Blackhawks reached the Final again in 1992. However, they lost in four games. It would be a while before they made it back.

STAN MIKITA

Bobby Hull was Chicago's leading goal-scorer in the 1960s. But right on his heels was center Stan Mikita. And Mikita was often the player who set up Hull for his goals. Hull himself said Mikita was the best hockey player in the world.

Mikita never played hockey as a child in Czechoslovakia. He discovered the game when he moved to Canada at the age of eight. Mikita grew to be just 5-foot-9. But he was tough for his size, and he could take a hit. He also helped popularize curved stick blades. Today, these blades are used by nearly all hockey players.

Mikita was the playmaker that made the Hawks go. When he retired, he ranked second on Chicago's list of most career goals. But he ranked first in assists and total points. In 2011, Mikita and Hull were both honored with statues outside the team's home arena.

Stan Mikita spent his entire 22-year
career with the Black Hawks.

4

Blackhawks center Jonathan Toews helped usher in a new era of excellence for the team.

A NEW DYNASTY

In 1983, Arthur Wirtz's son Bill took over as the team's owner. Bill Wirtz was often accused of not investing enough money in star players. And he refused to have home games broadcast on TV. Wirtz thought fans wouldn't buy tickets if they could watch the game for free on TV.

His strategy didn't work. The Hawks lost so often that many fans no longer bothered to show up.

However, those losses had a bright side. The Hawks got high draft picks. In 2006, Chicago used the third overall pick on center Jonathan Toews. The next year, the Hawks chose winger Patrick Kane first overall.

Kane and Toews joined a core of young, promising players. Toews became the team captain. Kane became one of the best playmakers in the NHL. Duncan Keith and Brent Seabrook locked down the defense.

Bill Wirtz's son Rocky took over in 2007. He quickly reversed his father's TV policy. Fans all across Chicago couldn't wait to tune in to watch their exciting young team. And in 2010, the Hawks

Patrick Kane lifts the Stanley Cup after scoring the championship-winning goal in 2010.

made it all the way to the Stanley Cup Final. Kane scored the Cup-winning goal in Game 6. That ended a 49-year streak without a title.

Best of all, the Hawks were just getting started. After their amazing comeback in the 2013 Final, the Hawks played for another Cup in 2015. This time, they won it on home ice. It was the first time they had done that since 1938.

OUTDOOR HOCKEY

The Blackhawks played in the second edition of the NHL Winter Classic. The outdoor game took place at Chicago's Wrigley Field in 2009. The Hawks went on to play in the annual game three more times over the next 11 years. That was the most of any team. However, outdoor hockey didn't seem to suit the Hawks. They lost all four games.

In the 2020–21 season, Blackhawks forward Alex DeBrincat led the team with 32 goals.

Unfortunately, the Hawks couldn't afford to keep all of their star players. Only Toews and Kane were left by 2021. But that was enough for fans to believe in another championship run.

CHICAGO BLACKHAWKS
QUICK STATS

FOUNDED: 1926

STANLEY CUP CHAMPIONSHIPS: 6 (1934, 1938, 1961, 2010, 2013, 2015)

KEY COACHES:

- Billy Reay (1963–76): 516 wins, 335 losses, 161 ties
- Joel Quenneville (2008–18): 452 wins, 249 losses, 96 overtime losses

HOME ARENA: United Center (Chicago, IL)

MOST CAREER POINTS: Stan Mikita (1,467)

MOST CAREER GOALS: Bobby Hull (604)

MOST CAREER ASSISTS: Stan Mikita (926)

MOST CAREER SHUTOUTS: Tony Esposito (74)

Stats are accurate through the 2020–21 season.

GLOSSARY

ASSISTS
Passes, rebounds, or deflections that result in goals.

CAPTAIN
A team's leader.

CENTER
A forward who typically plays in the middle of the offensive zone.

DRAFT
An event that allows teams to choose new players coming into the league.

ERA
A period of time in history.

PLAYOFFS
A set of games to decide a league's champion.

SLAP SHOT
A shot in which a player winds up and slaps the puck with great force.

WINGER
A forward who typically plays to the side of the net in the offensive zone.

TO LEARN MORE

BOOKS

Graves, Will. *Patrick Kane: Hockey Superstar*. Burnsville, MN: Press Room Editions, 2020.

Omoth, Tyler. *A Superfan's Guide to Pro Hockey Teams*. North Mankato, MN: Capstone Press, 2018.

Zweig, Eric. *Chicago Blackhawks*. New York: Crabtree Publishing Company, 2018.

MORE INFORMATION

To learn more about the Chicago Blackhawks, go to **pressboxbooks.com/AllAccess**.

These links are routinely monitored and updated to provide the most current information available.

INDEX